Original title:
Vineyard Visions

Copyright © 2025 Creative Arts Management OÜ
All rights reserved.

Author: Clara Whitfield
ISBN HARDBACK: 978-1-80566-756-8
ISBN PAPERBACK: 978-1-80566-826-8

The Grapes' Gentle Lament

Oh, squished and smashed, we softly cry,
Our juice escapes to the sky.
With every stomp, we giggle loud,
In our wrinkled skins, we feel so proud.

The barrels roll, they make us shake,
Oh, the jokes we have—what fun to make!
We dream of parades, oh so divine,
When we'll finally transform into wine.

Moonlit Maturation

Under moon's glow, we start to dance,
In the night breeze, we take a chance.
We whisper tales of days gone by,
As owls hoot softly, oh my, oh my!

The stars wink down, they know our fate,
To end in a bottle, oh how great!
But for now, we'll party with the owls,
Dancing our way through the midnight prowls.

Seasons of the Wine

In spring, we sprout, feeling so spry,
The bees buzz by with a curious eye.
In summer's heat, we bask and tease,
As ants throw parties beneath the leaves.

Autumn arrives with crunch underfoot,
Fall harvest time, oh what a hoot!
We race to ripen, we race through time,
Hoping for glory in the coming rhyme.

Tales from the Tasting Room

In the tasting room, we gather 'round,
Pouring our stories, making a sound.
"Is that a hint of berry?" someone will shout,
While others ponder, with eyes wide about.

We compete for the prize of best bouquet,
Crafting our stories in whimsical ways.
Laughter bubbles as glasses clink,
In this lovely space, we share and drink.

Sipping Through Seasons

In spring we sip on laughter,
With flowers in our glass,
The sun is bright, our hearts are light,
Let's raise a toast to sass.

In summer, grapes like trouble,
Come rolling down the hill,
With every thud, we squeal and shrug,
And drink another swill.

Autumn brings the harvest glee,
With barrels stacked like chairs,
We trip and fall while swiping small,
Our laughter fills the airs.

Winter's here, the chill sets in,
But spirits stay quite high,
We snuggle close and share a boast,
While sipping from the sly.

Soil and Soul

Digging deep with giggles,
Dirt under every nail,
The worms throw parties down below,
While we just sip and sail.

The grapes are rolling laughter,
As roots begin to play,
"You'll never guess," the soil jest,
"Who's coming out today!"

With every pour, a story grows,
Of shenanigans and cheer,
We toast to dirt, the silly flirt,
And sip away our fear.

So here's to life, that tangled strife,
In fields both wild and bold,
Where soil and soul make joy unroll,
And tales of fun are told.

The Craft of the Vine

Pressing grapes with silly grace,
A stomping dance ensues,
With laughter loud, we join the crowd,
In clogs and mismatched shoes.

Barrels roll like tumbling jokes,
A punchline's packed away,
With every sip, we start to trip,
On punchlines we can play.

Fermentation's bubbling fun,
As bubbles burst with cheer,
The craft takes flight, the jokes ignite,
And laughter fills our year.

So raise a glass, don't let it pass,
To craft that sparks delight,
In every vine, a twist of time,
Where fun meets every night.

Tales from Tannins

In shadowed corners, whispers blend,
    Of tannins bold and bright,
The stories flow, with every show,
    We sip and share our plight.

The castle walls hold secrets tight,
    While ghosts of grapes take flight,
They swirl around, with joyful sound,
    As we toast to the night.

Each vintage holds a different tale,
    Of antics rich and grand,
We clink our glasses in raucous blazes,
    And giggle hand in hand.

So come, pour out your giggly heart,
    With tales of vast delight,
In every drop, let laughter hop,
    And dance through the dim light.

Bunches of Memories

In the sun, the grapes do sway,
Unruly bunches in disarray.
A sip of joy, a splash of play,
Who knew they'd start a cabernet fray?

With every stomp, a squish and pop,
Careful now, let's not drop!
A dance of laughter, never stop,
As we make wine for the hop and bop!

Old barrels whisper tales of cheer,
Of grapes that wished to persevere.
A vintage laugh, a taste to steer,
With every toast, we draw near.

So raise your glass, let spirits soar,
For every grape, there's so much more.
A telling jest behind the door,
In every drop, our hearts encore.

Twilight Over the Trellis

As twilight's brush strokes the sky,
Grapes giggle as they pass by.
The harvest moon gives a sly hi,
While critters sneak for a late-night pie.

The crickets' tune, a quiet jest,
Whispers of grapes who've failed the test.
"Oops, I spilled," one claims with zest,
As laughter fills the evening's rest.

The shadows dance on the vine's embrace,
Each glint of light, a playful chase.
The joys of nature, a silly grace,
In this grape-filled, starry space.

So let's toast to fun, with no regrets,
For grapes and jokes, we'll never forget.
In the twilight glow, our hearts beget,
A world of laughter, no room for fret!

The Art of Fermentation

In barrels deep, the secrets swirl,
Yeast on a mission, taking a twirl.
Bubbles rise as giggles unfurl,
Who knew winemaking was such a whirl?

A splash of this, a dash of that,
"Oops, is that a cat?" someone spat.
The art of fermentation, where's the mat?
Playful spirits, oh imagine that!

With every sip, a story brews,
Of wild adventures and grape-filled blues.
A toast to blunders, our favorite news,
And sips that bring us vibrant hues.

So let's uncork the night with glee,
For each drop tells a tale carefree.
In the art of fun, we shall decree,
That laughter's the best wine, can't you see?

Beyond the Arbor

Beyond the arbor, adventures call,
Grapes in sunglasses, having a ball.
A squirrel sneaks in, just a small brawl,
As laughter echoes, a vine-woven hall.

Picnics thrive in leafy embrace,
With cheese that dares to run the race.
The grapes giggle, "Let's pick up the pace!"
As berry buddies join the chase.

In shadows cast by twinkle lights,
Grapes dance wildly, under the nights.
Each clink of glass, our spirits ignite,
Creating joy with every bite.

So gather 'round, let's toast the crew,
To silly moments, both old and new.
Beyond the arbor, laughter grew,
In every drop, a friendship true.

Bursting with Sunlit Flavor

Grapes giggle in the breeze,
They dance in clusters, tease and squeeze.
A jolly bunch in shades of green,
Chasing sunlight, quite a scene.

With every squish, a burst of cheer,
Their juicy laughter fills the air.
Frogs in ties and ants in shoes,
Join the party, raise their views.

Bottles pop like birthday fests,
Wine glasses cheer, we're all guests.
Sipping joy, we toast the day,
In this merry grape ballet.

Hiccups follow every sip,
Dance those vines, let laughter rip.
From rind to glass, the fun won't cease,
In this sweet, sunburst feast.

The Art of the Vintage

A painter with a grapevine brush,
Swirls of purple, no need to rush.
He spills some juice on canvas bare,
For art's sake, he doesn't care.

A cork pops like a party start,
Cheese and crackers play their part.
The vintage speaks, a cheeky grin,
Whispering secrets of the bin.

Sipping slowly, tasting time,
Froggish glee in every rhyme.
Each swirl reveals a funny phase,
Cellar tales of grand old days.

When art meets grapes in fruity jest,
The barrel laughs, it's truly blessed.
Corked up joy in every pour,
Raise a glass, let's taste some more!

Dreams Fermenting in Oak

Whispers swirl in the wooden core,
Where dreams rest easy, never a bore.
Stirring bubbles, secrets leak,
In this nook, the grapes all speak.

Barrels roll with a jig and jive,
Wooden walls keep dreams alive.
Each sip brings tales of grapes gone wild,
Crafting stories, sweet and mild.

The oak, it chuckles, full of glee,
An ancient soul, witty as can be.
A swirl of flavor, a dash of fun,
In this wood, the pranks are spun.

Pour it out, a tipple of luck,
Here in the casks, no one feels stuck.
With laughter rising like the steam,
Every bottle births a dream.

Nature's Liquid Canvas

Nature spills her vibrant hues,
In every drop, a laugh ensues.
Poured from jugs, life flows like art,
Each swirl and sip, a joyful heart.

Here comes the sun with a painter's hand,
Splashing colors across the land.
Leaves chuckle in the gentle breeze,
While bugs debate the best of cheese.

A grape-stomp dance, oh what a sight,
Gooey feet bring cheerful fright.
Sipping joy like it's a game,
In this canvas, wild and tame.

So grab your glass, don't let it slip,
Join the fun, take a joyful trip.
In nature's art, we find our bliss,
With every pour, we share a kiss.

Savoring the Sunset

The grapes are plumped, the night is near,
With laughter echoing, we sip the cheer.
A picnic spread with cheese and bread,
The sun dips low, the sky's a spread.

A raccoon steals our pie, oh what a mess,
We chase him off, but he's still a pest.
With wine-stained shirts and candied frowns,
The sunset's glow makes us all clowns.

Tasting the Tides

With barrels stacked by the shore so bright,
We taste the sea, while the moon's in sight.
A fish flip-flops right into our cup,
Should we drink it down? We say, "What's up?"

The seaweed swirls with a zesty twang,
A mermaid sings, and our laughter clangs.
Waves tickle toes, we splash with delight,
Who needs a cork? We'll drink it outright!

Enchantment of the Vineyard

In fields of green, where the giggles bloom,
A grape rolls past, it must've found room.
We dance with bottles, we twirl in style,
That comical grape, it makes us all smile.

The frogs serenade from the old oak tree,
While raccoons play band, as lively as can be.
The corks pop loud, like a story we weave,
In this wacky world, joy's what we believe.

Lament of the Lost Harvest

Oh where are the fruits that should hang with glee?
   The scarecrow's on break, with no eyes to see.
   The squirrels conspire, they're sneaky and sly,
     While we sit and ponder, "Oh my, oh my!"

The pumpkins have fled, in a dance gone awry,
   The apples have formed a rebellious tie.
   With giggles we gather the few fruits that stay,
     And toast to the chaos, "Hip-hip-hurray!"

Nectar of the Earth

In fields of grapes where laughter grows,
The squirrels dance with silly toes.
A pickle floats on a wineglass wave,
While ants hold parties, oh so brave.

The sun wears shades, a cheerful sight,
Bottles whistle tunes, full of delight.
The bees are buzzing jokes galore,
While birds recount their tales, encore!

Beneath the vines, a cat does nap,
While raccoons plot their sneaky trap.
Wine stains giggle on the floor,
As happy grapes cry out for more!

A toast to laughter, let joy commence,
With every sip, let's raise the suspense.
For in this land of grapey cheer,
The best of jokes are bottled here!

Sipping Summer's Essence

With sunny hats and picnic flair,
We sip delight from the open air.
Grapes wear shades, the sun is strong,
As we spill jokes in a silly thong.

A cork pops off with a comic shot,
While birds tune in for a wobbly plot.
The juice flows thick with giggling streams,
We float in laughter, lost in dreams.

A worm in shade writes quirky notes,
As frogs wear crowns on their royal coats.
The bottles waltz beneath the trees,
While crickets plot their funny tease.

With cups held high, we cheer the glee,
As shadows dance in jubilee.
This summer sip, oh how divine,
We laugh and sip our frothy wine!

Roots Beneath the Soil

Beneath the roots where secrets lie,
Worms throw parties, oh my, oh my!
They boast of treasures buried deep,
While moles create a raucous beep.

Rocks tell tales of ancient fun,
As laughter bubbles, one by one.
The earthworms twist in disco lights,
Inviting bugs to join in flights.

A grape takes flight on a breeze so bold,
Telling stories of the sun's warm gold.
A dance-off starts near the old oak,
Roots tremble under every joke.

In secret soil, the giggles rise,
As nature plots a grand surprise.
With every sip from this earthy toy,
We find the laughter, we find the joy!

Emergence of the Vintage

From barrels deep, a trumpets' call,
"Here comes the vintage! Go jump and sprawl!"
Glasses clink in a friendly fray,
As grapes report their funny play.

A bottle sings, it rolls and dances,
While hiccuping corks take funny chances.
The labels cheer, "We're one of a kind!"
As laughter flows like a glass of rind.

Old vines chat over tales of war,
Of grapes who dreamed of something more.
With every glass raised to the sky,
We celebrate with a giggling sigh.

As barrels roll in jovial glee,
Every sip honors creativity.
In this embrace of fruity fun,
The vintage laughs – let's sip and run!

Sips of Solitude

A grape once dreamed of being fine,
In a bottle, oh how divine!
But he tripped on a cork one day,
Now he rolls and just wants to play.

Underneath the sun's hot vibe,
Fellow grapes sing in the jive.
They talk of merlot and of pinot,
While I sip on something quite so-so.

A beetle stole my glassy prize,
In a twist, he won the size.
Now he's king of the red parade,
As I laugh at my failed charade.

So raise a toast to mishaps grand,
Join the laughter, take my hand.
For in the world of fermented laughs,
Even sips can spark new gaffes.

Elysian Ambrosia

In a land where grapes all jest,
Some claim to be the very best.
But one wore shades and took a dive,
Said, "This is how I come alive!"

With every sip, a giggle flows,
As sticky juice drips off your nose.
The critics frown, but who would care,
When dancing grapes are everywhere?

A cabernet slipped on a rind,
Declared, "This party's one of a kind!"
He twirled so fast, he caught a breeze,
And laughed away the grown-up tease.

Pour a glass and let it spill,
Laughter's funny, what a thrill!
Ambrosia served with a side of cheer,
Grapes unite; it's fun, my dear!

The Heart's Fermentation

A bottle sits with hope inside,
Dreaming of the joy worldwide.
But it hiccups, oh what a sound,
Turns out, that joy was out of bounds!

The cork was tight, the bubbles bust,
In whirls of laughter, find the trust.
Hearts ferment in joyful tunes,
With each mistake, we share great boons!

A crush that danced upon the floor,
Said, "Why not let our spirits soar?"
In every sip, a story's spun,
A clumsy dance becomes our fun.

So join the heart that's bubbling loud,
Let's toast to life, we're all so proud.
For fermentation fills the air,
With bubbly joys and no despair!

Journey of the Juice

In barrels deep, the juices dream,
Trips and spills make quite the scene.
Each grape has tales of wacky flight,
From harvest days to starry nights.

A rogue grape rolled off the shelf,
Said, "I need to find myself!"
He landed in a laughing crew,
Together, they made quite the stew!

With each sip, wild stories flow,
Of pranks and pickles, and a show.
Who knew the juice could bring such fun?
With every laugh, we've surely won!

So as we sip, just let it go,
Each bottle hides a tale to show.
In the journey of sweet delight,
We find our joy, both day and night.

Twilight over the Trellis

In the dusk, the grapes are shy,
Hiding from the clownish fly.
Bottles jostle in the breeze,
As I trip over roots with ease.

The moon snickers, hanging low,
As I dance to the vine's soft flow.
Laughing at my grape-stomp move,
'Tis a sight, not much to prove.

Crickets play their nightly tune,
While I search for lost balloon.
Each laugh echoes in the night,
Underneath the twinkling light.

With each sip, I tell a tale,
Of the night when grapes went pale.
Twilight wraps us in its cheer,
As I share my tipsy leer.

Uncorking Dreams

Pop the cork, hear the cheer,
Dreams uncorked for us to hear.
Laughter bubbles in the glass,
As I trip, I cannot pass.

Pouring out my wildest dream,
It sparkles, or so it seems.
Grapes whisper jokes, quite absurd,
'Was that a bird or just a nerd?'

My friend spills wine upon the floor,
We giggle, 'What's a little more?'
Each splash lands like our lost hope,
We craft joy, tied with a rope.

In this chaos, we find glee,
As a cork flies, straight at me.
Uncorking fears with every sip,
On this merry, rolling trip.

The Scent of Fermentation

Oh, the stench of dreams gone wild,
Like a toddler's feet, quite riled.
Barrels bubble with delight,
As I ponder, 'Is that a fight?'

Grapes giggle in fermentation,
Creating quite the sensation.
As I sniff, I'm hit by fate,
Beneath a hat that's far too straight.

The aroma fills the air,
Drunken bees join in the fair.
Dancing grapes and bees collide,
In this sweet, sticky ride.

What a scent, I'm not quite sure,
Is that breakfast or a cure?
Fuzzed thoughts drift in the mist,
Wondering which ones I've kissed.

A Palette of Purples

Purple hues come out to play,
Painting smiles along the way.
With each blob from careless hands,
We create grapes in strange bands.

I slipped on juice, oops, what a mess!
Grapes chuckle, 'Now that's finesse!'
The table's set for a silly feast,
As I wiggle like a grape beast.

Swirling colors, oh so bright,
Dancing shadows in the light.
With tipsy brushes, we draw dreams,
On canvas soaked with winey creams.

A palette full, we raise a cheer,
With grape-shaped hats, quite the gear.
In this art, we found our bliss,
A grape escape, we can't miss!

Beneath the Twining Vines

Beneath the green, where grapes conspire,
I found a bunch that spoke of desire.
"Pick me, pick me!" they gave a shout,
But I just laughed and wandered about.

The sunbeam tickled, the bugs did dance,
Each grape had a story, each leaf a chance.
One whispered secrets, one told a joke,
I raised my glass, said, "Here's to hope!"

The shadows stretched as the day grew late,
I joined a grape, we shared our fate.
"What's the point?" I asked with cheer,
"Life is a party, let's drink and steer!"

So if you wander where the fruit is bold,
Don't take it too serious, be merry not cold.
For under those twining, a laughter resides,
In every sip, a joy that abides.

The Dance of the Grape Leaves

The grape leaves flutter in whimsical glee,
Swirling around like a drunken bee.
They tango with breezes, they twirl and spin,
Mocking the groundlings who just can't win.

A leaf took a tumble, a somersault dip,
Land on a grape, said, "Let's take a trip!"
"The view's better here!" the grape leaf yelled,
As every fruit blushed, no secret held.

The sun watched in awe, the clouds threw a glance,
Wondering if grapes knew how to prance.
With roots deep in soil, they giggled and flipped,
Life in the grove was a funny little script.

So join in the dance, where nature convenes,
Where grapes make the music and leaves find their dreams.
In the laughter of fruits, joy simply flows,
A vineyard of giggles, where anything goes!

Secrets in the Soil

Beneath the earth, where whispers play,
The roots exchange tales in a hidden ballet.
One said, "I'm shy, but I know the scoop!"
Another replied, "Come join the loop!"

There's laughter in dirt, and gossip galore,
As worms take the stage, and weeds ask for more.
"Did you hear about grape, got a bit too tipsy?"
The roots chuckled low, like, "That's kinda risky!"

The earth has its secrets, not all are so clean,
Dirt on the grapes that will never be seen.
Each clump holds a story, each rock has a laugh,
As roots weave together a fantastic path.

So let's dig a bit deeper, have fun with our toil,
For buried beneath, is the heart of the soil.
In the laughter of roots, we all intertwine,
In the secrets they keep, there's a joy so divine!

Bunches of Time

I tried to count moments like grapes on a vine,
But time slipped away—oh, isn't it fine?
Each bunch held a memory, a giggle, a grin,
A bottle of laughter where joy would begin.

"Yesterday's grapes, all wrinkled and sweet,
Tasted like wisdom, oh, they're quite a treat!"
Said a young sprout, still green with a dream,
"But aging is tricky, or so it would seem!"

With glasses raised high, we toasted our past,
To moments well lived, and the fun that they cast.
For time's just a harvest, a quirky delight,
Each sip is a story that brings us to light.

So cherish each bunch, both tender and old,
For the laughter we gather is a treasure untold.
In the vineyards of life, where all intertwine,
Every drop, every chuckle is genuinely fine!

Tendrils of Time

Grapes hang low, a silly sight,
Bouncing in the sun, oh what a fright!
Weaving tales of lush delight,
As squirrels steal sips in broad daylight.

With every swirl of fruity cheer,
The jester's jokes, we hold so dear.
The clock spins round, in goofy cheer,
Time slips by, with every beer.

Oh, beetles dance like they know best,
In this green realm, they jest and jest.
Pour another glass, it's time for rest,
Grape-stompers claim they're quite the zest!

In the midst of laughter, care we find,
Life's too short, with grapes entwined.
So raise a glass to silly grind,
In this grape-laden dream, we're all aligned!

Fables from the Ferment

In barrels deep, the secrets sleep,
Whispered tales the grapes do keep.
Bubbles giggle in the night air,
While corks pop with a daring flair.

Once a grape dreamed it could fly,
But stuck to earth with a woeful sigh.
Now it dances in a glass, oh my!
Fables from the ferment, passing by.

The spirits swirl, in mischievous play,
Laughing at the tipsy sway.
Each sip a legend, hip hooray!
Even the harvesters start to sway!

A boisterous tale of twists and turns,
In this grand jest, each heart yearns.
For laughter's drink, the spirit burns,
Let's raise a toast while the barrel churns!

The Echoing Harvest

Beneath the sun, we gather here,
With laughter ringing, oh so clear.
Baskets swinging, full of cheer,
Cracking jokes while downing beer.

Grapes ricochet off our toes,
The funky dance, everybody knows.
Everyone's spouting, funny prose,
As the sun dips low, and laughter grows.

With every stomp, the juice flies high,
Some chase grapes, oh my, oh my!
Grapevines chuckle, watching nearby,
The harvest sings with a silly sigh.

As night descends, we sip and sway,
In this wild romp, the worries fray.
The echoes of laughter softly play,
Harvesting joy at the end of day!

A Harvest of Hope

In rows of green, dreams unfold,
Grape by grape, tales of old.
With fingers crossed, the stories told,
The silliness we're yet to behold.

Jesters dance on leaves so bright,
While crickets chirp in sheer delight.
The harvest moon beams through the night,
Every bottle holds a spark of light.

Hope bounces in the sweetest wine,
Each sip a giggle, oh how divine!
Life's a party on this grapevine,
With every toast, our spirits entwine.

So here's to us, with hearts aglow,
Riding the waves of joy's warm flow.
In the laughter, let's take it slow,
For every harvest lets good vibes grow!

Grapes Beneath the Sun

Grapes are lounging, having fun,
Sunlight gleams on everyone.
A purple party, feeling fine,
They sip their juice, divine design.

Rolling down the gentle hill,
Making juice, what a thrill!
They laugh and dance, a fruity cheer,
While bees buzz in, quite near.

Under blue skies, oh what a scene,
Grapes in shorts, all looking keen.
From plump to squishy, they play a game,
Each one's a star, in their own fame.

Come on over, join the jam,
Grab a grape, and take a slam.
It's a harvest fest, with bursts of glee,
These silly fruits, wild and free.

Whispers of Ripened Clusters

Clusters gossip in the breeze,
Talking 'bout their summer leaves.
Plump ones share their juicy tales,
While smaller ones just wiggle their tails.

Chatting grapes, a merry crew,
Who knew they had so much to do?
They plot the best ways to delight,
Dream of parties every night.

Underneath the leafy shade,
They laugh at each escapade.
Sanctuary from the sun,
Ripened dreams for everyone.

With whispers soft, they tease and laugh,
Planning how to take a bath.
In a bowl, nice and grand,
Celebrating, hand-in-hand.

A Symphony of Sipping

Raise your glasses, let us cheer,
For the grapes that brought us here.
With every sip, a story flows,
Joyful tunes as laughter grows.

A splash of red, a dash of white,
Swirling flavors, pure delight.
Musical notes in every glass,
Grapes perform, they have the class.

With clinking sounds, they orchestrate,
Harmonies that captivate.
Each toast a verse, a dance, a song,
In this grape symphony, we all belong.

So join the feast, let's celebrate,
The magic found upon our plate.
Grapes together, what a sight,
Sipping tunes throughout the night.

Hues of Harvest Twilight

As twilight paints the skies with gold,
Grapes wear colors, bold and old.
From purples deep to greens so bright,
Each hue's a laugh, a sheer delight.

Chubby bunches begin to sway,
Beneath the stars, they frolic, play.
While shadows stretch upon the ground,
Grapes giggle softly, joy abound.

With every sunset, tales unfold,
Each grape a comedian, ever bold.
They recount days of the warm sun,
Where each found laughter's sweetest fun.

So here's to grapes, a colorful crew,
To the harvest hues and skies so blue.
Let the world toast with smiles and cheer,
For twilight laughter, let's all revere.

Memories Bottled

In a barrel, I fall and roll,
A corked-up dream, that's rock and scroll.
Grapes laugh softly, squished in cheer,
As winemakers dance with no fear.

Sipping laughter, we chase the sun,
Each glass a giggle, oh what fun!
Sticky fingers from spilled delight,
Toasted to life, it feels just right.

Each bottle whispers tales so sweet,
Of blunders past and tasty feats.
With every sip, the world grows tall,
As I recount my drunken brawl.

The cork pops off, oh what a sight!
Like juggling grapes in moonlit night.
Friends gather round, tales grow wild,
As childhood memories run reviled.

Verdant Embrace

In leafy dresses, grapes march proud,
Tickling the sky, beneath a cloud.
A vine wraps 'round like an old friend,
Whispering secrets it cannot blend.

Bunches giggle, swinging in breeze,
While fermentation brings them to tease.
A summer's embrace, playful and bright,
Turning even the meek into light.

With sips of joy, we sway and spin,
A grape soda pop, let the games begin!
Corkscrew antics, a party galore,
As vines and laughter twist and explore.

Under the sun, we dance and hop,
With each jolly pop, there's no stop.
The fruit and the fun, a merry sprawl,
In this green paradise, we thrive for all.

The Flavor of Freedom

Out in the fields, wild grapes play,
A fruity festival, hip hip hooray!
Each splash of juice, a giggly burst,
To seize the day is a must, we thirst!

With baskets full, we race and prance,
Chasing bubbles as they dance.
Every sip's a ticket to dream,
Riding waves of bubbly cream.

Toast to the laughter, toast to the fun,
Dancing round like a lively bun.
In each glass, a dose of glee,
We toast to freedom, you and me!

Pinot, Merlot, each edge a thrill,
Like socks on floors that wanna spill.
With every flavor, our hearts take flight,
Let's clink our glasses under moonlight.

Honeyed Hues of Autumn

Leaves of gold, a drunken swirl,
As honey drips, we dance and twirl.
Grapes grow fat in the autumn air,
Wobbling cheeks, we just don't care.

Cider's laughing, so warm and bright,
With hints of spice, it feels just right.
Swirling mugs in an endless jest,
We celebrate every silly quest.

The harvest feast, oh what a sight!
Pumpkins rolling, a lively fight.
Jugs of laughter, barrels of cheer,
As autumn whispers, "Drink up, my dear!"

Sticky fingers and joyful grins,
With every gulp, the fun begins.
As leaves fall down in a swirling mess,
We toast to the sweet, and nothing less!

Moonlit Grape Tales

Under the moon, grapes dance in a line,
A cheeky raccoon sips on some wine.
Whispering secrets, the barrels agree,
That night's best stories always come free.

Frogs in tuxedos serenade the night,
While owls hoot loudly, it's quite a sight.
The stars watch in laughter, a cosmic surprise,
As tipsy shadows join in the cries.

A squirrel in shades claims the best grape,
With tales of the harvest, fits to escape.
Every grape has a story, so juicy and ripe,
In this moonlit garden, all is hype.

So raise a glass high, toast to the night,
Where grapes and giggles create pure delight.
Each sip is a story, a chuckle, a cheer,
In this whimsical realm, let's all persevere!

Varietal Vignettes

In rows of color, the grapevines sing,
Stories of mishaps and silly bling.
The cabernet whispered, "I'm a big deal!"
While the muscat rolled eyes, "What's your appeal?"

A barrel of secrets, bubbling with glee,
Told tales of a party thrown by the bee.
Dancing all night, with nectar so sweet,
They swayed and they jived, not missing a beat.

The chardonnay giggled, "I'm fancy, you see!"
But the zinfandel yelled, "You're just like me!"
Together they laughed, in a playful spat,
For wine's just a drink—when you're smiling like that!

So swirl your glass gently, let stories abound,
In this riot of grapes, joy's always found.
Raise your voice high, let the fun take its flight,
With varietals laughing till morning's first light!

Through the Oak's Embrace

Under the oak's arms, grapes gather close,
Swapping wild tales, and sipping, they toast.
"One grape fell down, rolled straight for the creek!"
Said the old vine, chuckling, "What a cheek!"

The children of vines played peek-a-boo games,
A duck waddled by, calling them names.
While shadows played tricks in the cool evening breeze,
The grapes cracked up at such comic unease.

A burly old fox, wearing a hat,
Joined the grape party, and imagine that!
He told them of dreams that had slipped from the vine,
While they snickered and snorted, their laughter divine.

So let's raise a cheer under this ancient bough,
For the hilarity of life, and the joy in the now.
With each burst of laughter, the world fades away,
Through the oak's embrace, we'll all choose to play!

A Stroll by the Vines

Strolling through rows of green, so divine,
Grapes gabbing gossip, like it's all fine.
"Did you hear about berry wearing a crown?"
"Who knew such a grape could be such a clown?"

A ladybug joined in, wearing a bow,
"Excuse me, dear grapes, can you lay low?"
They jested and jived, like a vine party scene,
In the land of the laughter, where all was serene.

The farmer just chuckled, ahead on the lane,
While the phantoms of grapes spiced up the mundane.
"Keep it down, will you? I've work to be done!"
But the grapes just winked, and said, "This is fun!"

With each plump bunch, a giggle would spread,
As nature conspired, painting joy red.
So join us in jest, as we merrily sway,
In a stroll by the vines, let's laugh the day away!

Reflections in the Glass

A swirl of red, a splash of white,
In my glass, the world feels right.
I sip and grin, my worries fade,
Are those my jokes, or simply shade?

The bottle's label, oh what a sight,
I swear it smiled before the night.
With each full pour, my laughter grows,
Now I confuse my friend with prose!

The Aroma of Dusk

As dusk descends, the scents arise,
A whiff of grapes and some surprise.
I sniffed a vine, said, "Is that me?"
The grapes just smiled, "That's not for free!"

With every breath, a giggle blooms,
As to the cellar, I set my dooms.
The air is ripe, it cannot lie,
Did that grape just wink? Oh my!

Glistening Grapes at Dawn

The morning sun, it plays a game,
With glistening grapes, oh what a fame!
I tried to dance, so light and free,
But tripped on vines—now grape juice on me!

A ladybug laughs, perched on a leaf,
"I swear these grapes, they hold belief.
For every splash, a story untold,
Of drunken nights and friendships bold!"

The Dance of the Leaves

The leaves are swirling, a messy waltz,
I join the jig, oh what a false!
I twirl and tumble, crash to the ground,
Who knew the earth could spin around?

With each bright gust, I laugh and squeal,
Are those grape leaves or a surreal deal?
As they bow low in playful glee,
I wonder if they're laughing at me!

Grape Stains on the Heart

In a world of swirling grapes,
I tripped and fell, oh what a fate!
My heart now bears a purple mark,
Like art, but funnier, oh what a spark!

I swayed beneath the autumn breeze,
With fruity visions that tease and please.
A sip, a slosh, a splash so grand,
Oops! Did I spill? It's all unplanned!

The sun shines bright on tattered shoes,
I dance with joy, then trip—what a ruse!
Sticky fingers til I roam,
In this jolly grape-filled home!

But if you laugh at my grape-splashed soul,
Join the fun, let's rock 'n roll!
For life is sweeter with a dash of cheer,
Here's to the stains we can wear all year!

The Elegance of the Oak

Oh, the oak stands tall, dressed to impress,
With arms stretched wide in a fancy dress.
But beams one day—you really won't guess,
It spilled the wine, oh, what a mess!

Dressed in elegance, but clumsy still,
Swirling in laughter, oh what a thrill!
The squirrels laugh at their neighbor's blunder,
Under the sun—a true comedy under!

The acorns chuckle, they roll and spin,
As trunks attempt a waltz—a spin-win.
Beneath the branches, joy takes its claim,
With oak so grand, we forget the shame!

So here's to the oaks with wine on their leaves,
In comical outfits that anybody believes!
Let's raise a glass to those who can cheer,
For elegance comes with a dash of silly beer!

Whimsy in the Wine

In a glass of red, a world distilled,
Dancing bubbles, oh what a thrill!
Each sip, a chuckle, a silly face,
As grapes engage in a wobbly race!

Corks pop loud, like fireworks bright,
Every toast turns giggles to flight.
Laughter rings out over the vines,
While glasses clink in cheerful lines!

A swirl of white, and giggles ensue,
The sommelier trips—now what will he do?
With each playful sip, let mischief ignite,
In the land of grapes, all feels just right!

So gather 'round, let the fun unwine,
Experiencing joy in each sip of wine.
Raise a toast to the laughter we share,
In this whimsical toast, we haven't a care!

Vision of the Vintner

The vintner peeks through grapes galore,
  With wild ideas that we can't ignore.
He spills his dreams on the barrel's edge,
  Each plan a joke, but we pledge!

He claims, "I'll make a sparkling delight,
With bubbles that jump and take flight!"
But sometimes they pop, oh what a scene,
  Chasing the fizz in a wacky routine!

Visions of vines and dances they weave,
While he dreams of flavors we can't believe.
With laughter echoing deep in the vale,
  A fruity parade, non-stop without fail!

So here's to the vintner, so merry and bright,
With each funny mishap, he reignites light.
In this grape-filled world, let joy be the aim,
  For even the oaky, can play a fun game!

Tapestry of Terroir

Grapes in rows like soldiers stand,
Wearing sunlight, wine in hand.
They giggle as they swell and freeze,
Whispering secrets in the breeze.

Oh, merry vines, with twisted glee,
Dancing under the old oak tree.
A grapevine tale, a jester's jest,
In the land of wine, we're all the best!

The earth is thick with jokes and puns,
Some grapes just bask in the warm sun.
Others plot a juicy prank,
While sipping nectar at the rank.

In the vineyard's heart, dear friends abound,
Finding laughter in the ground.
So raise your glass and share a cheer,
In this grape-filled world, there's nothing to fear!

The Harvest Moon's Serenade

Under the moon, the grapes prepare,
To make a wine that's rare and fair.
But some get tipsy, it's a riot,
They stumble and laugh, oh what a diet!

The owls are hooting 'til they're sore,
As fruit does tumble, roll, and more.
No need for glasses, we see clear,
Wine doesn't ask well, it just wants cheer.

A cork pops off with quite a shout,
For a grape can't sip if it's knocked out.
Bottles dance like they've got feet,
What a fine way to share a treat!

So we gather round with glee and space,
For laughter is the true outpace.
Under the harvest moon's gaze so bright,
We toast to grapes in the silver light!

A Symphony of Sangiovese

Sangiovese, sweet and bold,
Plays a tune that's fun to hold.
A grape that twirls and sings at night,
Cracking jokes, oh what delight!

In barrels wide, they joke around,
Making notes that are profound.
Some are high, and some are low,
The chorus leaves us all aglow.

A bunch gets tipsy, starts a fight,
Over who gets the last sip right.
But laughter fills the vine-filled air,
When charm is mixed with juicy flair!

So let us dance with the grape brigade,
To the sweet serenade they made.
Raise your glass and join the spree,
In this symphony, we all agree!

Shadows of the Grapevine

In the twilight, shadows play,
Grapes whisper low, come join the fray.
They tickle each other with leafy hands,
In this madcap land where giggles stand.

A sip of joy brings forth the muse,
Where corks pop off and minds amuse.
Grapevines stretch to the evening sky,
As the laughter rolls and spirits fly.

Bottles gather, tales do spin,
The grapes unite to let fun win.
Even the owls can't help but snort,
At the grape antics, their nightly sport.

So let's linger in the vine-lit night,
With cheer and glee, our hearts so light.
In shadows cast by moon and wine,
We find our joy, pure and divine!

Notes from the Grape Harvest

Grapes in buckets, oh what a sight,
Wobbling like jello, it's quite a delight.
Sipping the juice, we laugh out loud,
These little berries sure make us proud.

With each squished step, our shoes stick tight,
Grape juice splatters, oh what a fright!
We dance on the vines, our hearts in tune,
The grapes send whispers beneath the moon.

Nature's sweetness spills out in cheer,
Friends all around, not a worry or fear.
We pick and we giggle, oh what a mess,
The vineyard's our stage, we're truly blessed.

When harvest is done, we'll raise a toast,
To the grapes that brought us together the most.
With laughter and joy poured right from the cup,
Here's to the memories that fill us up!

A Journey Through the Rows

We wander through rows, in light so bright,
Each grape is a giggle, a pure delight.
Sun hats and laughter, a parade so grand,
With juice dribbling down, it's all unplanned.

The vines seem to whisper their silly tales,
Of wobbly feet and clumsy fails.
A grape on the ground gives us a scare,
But we just laugh; we haven't a care.

We skip and we hop, like children at play,
While birds in the trees make their own bouquet.
Here comes a bunch that looks really fine,
Oh, what a time to pick and dine!

Another sweet slip in this fruity spree,
Packed with delight, it's a rich jubilee.
We'll treasure these moments, so silly and bright,
Our journey through rows is pure delight!

The Language of the Vines

The vines have their secrets, we try to decode,
They giggle in whispers as we hit the road.
Each cluster is gossip, juicy and bold,
Tales of past summers in stories retold.

With leaves all a-flutter, they sing us a tune,
Beneath the bright sun and the glowing moon.
They speak of sweet drops, come have a taste,
In their merry company, we're never in haste.

A grape takes a tumble, oh what a scene,
It rolls down the row like it's part of a dream.
We chase it with laughter, slipping on dew,
The language of vines shows us something new.

So let's toast to the tales that each vine has spun,
And dance through the rows, oh it's so much fun!
With every sweet nibble and giggly cheer,
The language of vines is music to hear!

Secrets of the Soil

Beneath our feet, a story does hide,
Earth's giggles and chuckles, a secretive guide.
With worms as the crew in this earthy delight,
Soil is a party that goes every night.

The roots tickle gently, they wiggle with glee,
Doing the tango beneath you and me.
While rocks play the drums, oh what a band!
In the festival soil, we'll jive hand in hand.

"We grow the best grapes!" the daisies proclaim,
As we stomp on the ground in a silly old game.
Let's dig up the past, what can we find?
A treasure of laughter that's one of a kind!

So here's to the secrets that soil can keep,
Where laughter is buried, but never too deep.
In every sweet sip that the grape vines provide,
There's fun in the soil, let's enjoy the ride!

The Dreamer's Cellar

In a darkened room, the corkscrew's dance,
Bottles are singing, given the chance.
With a hiccup and giggle, I raise my glass,
To the tales of the grapes that time can't surpass.

Beneath dusty lights, the barrels do lean,
Whispering secrets, a comedic scene.
A couple of figs and a slice of brie,
I'm the king of the cellar, just pour it on me!

I stumble on boxes, my toes in a twist,
Every stumble's a step in my vino remix.
The labels may blur, but I'm never alone,
With laughter and bubbles, I'll call this my throne.

So here's to the nights spent in laughter and cheer,
In the dreamer's cellar, there's naught to fear.
With each merry sip, the world disappears,
And I sail through the waves of good-hearted cheers.

Blossoms in the Breeze

Picture the vines, they sway in the sun,
Tickled by breezes, oh what fun!
Petals flutter down like secret notes,
While bees do the tango in tiny boats.

A grape giggles softly, just hanging around,
Chasing the clouds that dance on the ground.
With each little drop that falls from the sky,
The flowers shout out, 'Oh my, oh my!'

Bacchus is laughing, his cup spilling low,
As I trip through the rows where the wild blossoms grow.

They tease me with colors, so vivid, so bright,
I'm lost in their chatter, what a comical sight!

So let all the blossoms cause mischief and cheer,
In this grape-laden land, joy's volunteer.
We'll dance with a vine, both silly and free,
In the breeze of good humor, where life feels so glee.

Echoes of the Grape

From the vineyard echoes a playful refrain,
Of grapes with a giggle, they're dancing in rain.
They chuckle and bounce as they ripen with grace,
In this world full of joy, there's never a race.

"Squash the day blues!" the cabernets shout,
With moments so rich, who could do without?
A splash of red wine, and the laughter will flow,
As the grapes share old stories from long, long ago.

The sauvignon sloshes with comedic flair,
Whispering secrets it's eager to share.
With a wink and a nod, the chardonnay sighs,
In the echoes of laughter, chill out or surprise!

A toast to the grape in its jovial role,
Launching the good times straight into the soul.
Here's to the jokes, both silly and great,
In this vine-soaked adventure, we celebrate fate.

A Canvas of Cabernet

Dripping, dabbing, a splashy delight,
A canvas unfolding in pure red delight.
I paint with my wine, oh what a scene,
Mixing mishaps with laughter, like a festive machine.

Brush strokes of merlot, chaotic yet neat,
As I create the masterpiece - oh, what a feat!
With a gulp and a giggle, I toss on some rhymes,
In the art of the grape, I'm defying all times.

The brushes are dancing, the bottles take flight,
Every drop tells a story, a novel in sight.
So here's to the chaos, the splatter of fun,
While the canvases echo, "We've only begun!"

In this swirling palette, I'm lost in delight,
With each sip and each stroke, my worries take flight.
So raise up your brush, let the laughter unfurl,
In the canvas of cabernet, let's paint our own world!

Shades of Vineyard Dreams

In rows they stand, hats askew,
Grapes whisper secrets, who knew?
Foot stomping's a sight to behold,
Juice flying like stories, bold!

Mice in the barrels, having a feast,
They party hard, to say the least.
Grape juice rivers, running wild,
Dancing grapes, the drunks beguiled!

When winsome wine meets sun's embrace,
A cork pops off, it's a wild race.
Bottles wobbled, laughter's sway,
Grape expectations lead us astray!

Oh, the dreams trapped in each vine,
Make merry the mishaps, toast with wine!
Pour another, let laughter gleam,
In our tipsy, tumbling dream!

The Fusion of Flavor

Grapes and giggles, a curious blend,
Mixing flavors, a twist to send.
Bubbles rise like jokes we share,
Puns fermenting in the air!

One sip brings a chuckle and grin,
A dash of spice makes the fun begin.
Grapefruit, peach, a twist so bright,
A sip too much? Now that's a fright!

Whirling around in a zesty dance,
Every gulp gives laughter a chance.
To tease the senses, watch them burst,
In the glass, flavors always thirst!

So raise your glass, have a taste,
In this wild fusion, nothing goes to waste.
Pour it easy, don't spill, it's key,
For a blend of fun – just wait and see!

Sip by Sip

A drop of red, a splash of green,
Sip by sip, the fun is seen.
The cork flew off, straight for a hat,
Who knew we'd be such acrobats?

Tasting notes make no sense today,
Is that chocolate or a twist of hay?
We swirl and snicker, who's in charge?
The grapes giggle, aren't they large?

Sipping slowly, oh what a chore,
Chasing the giggles, always wanting more.
Half the time, we spill it wide,
But that's just fun, we take in stride!

So gather 'round, let's take the plunge,
With every sip, it's a laughing lunge.
A fête of flavors, a silly spree,
In each glass, pure jubilee!

The Glory of Grapes

There once was a grape who dreamed to shine,
Joined the harvest, felt just divine.
With each crush, a comedy play,
Out popped the juice, hip-hip-hooray!

Purple orbs with dreams so vast,
Wishing to be the wine that lasts.
But too much stomp turned fancy thoughts,
Into giggles and fermented knots!

Grape-naps planned in the afternoon sun,
When they wake, it's all for fun.
Gathered in barrels, they giggle and sway,
Making fine juice for a silly day!

So here's to the grapes, the jesters of cheer,
Making us laugh with every sip near.
Raise your glasses, enjoy the jokes,
The glory of grapes, a dance for folks!

Echoes of Autumn's Bounty

The grapes all chatter, sip and sigh,
Beneath a cloud, those clouds roll by.
A dance of leaves, a rustle grows,
With every plop, the humor flows.

The squirrels throw parties, quite absurd,
With nuts as snacks, they mock the birds.
A harvest moon, the antics soar,
They toast with cider, shout for more!

The pumpkins giggle, lining the road,
A jolly crew, they share the load.
Side-splitting laughter, autumn's cheer,
While critters plot, the feast draws near.

So raise a glass to nature's jest,
In harvest time, we find our best.
With every laugh, the bounty grows,
In liquid joy, the spirit flows.

Nectar and Nature

The bees debate on who will land,
As blossoms swell, they make their plan.
With cha-cha wings and wiggly dance,
They sip the nectar—oh, what a chance!

The flowers giggle, spreading their scent,
To lure those bees, their base intent.
While butterflies tease with dazzling flair,
They flit and flutter, without a care.

A rogue grape rolled under the sun,
Declares, 'This year, I'm number one!'
But ants march in with tiny pride,
To snag the fruit, they won't abide.

So join the buzz, the playful strife,
In nature's realm, we share the life.
With sweetness dripping, laughter's call,
Every sip's a joy for all!

In the Shade of the Grapevines

Under the trellis, where whispers flow,
The grapes are gossiping, putting on a show.
With shades of green and sun-soaked dreams,
They plot their ways, or so it seems.

A chubby hen struts down the lane,
Clucking her tales of summer rain.
While critters laugh, they mock her pride,
'Your feathers weigh more than grapes inside!'

The squirrels spin tales of daring flight,
Hoping the wind will join their plight.
With leafy hats, they scheme and plot,
In this shady spot, their jokes are hot.

So raise a toast with laughter and glee,
To the veggies and fruits that aim to be free.
With humor ripe, we savor the tales,
In shady lounges, the joy prevails.

Liquid Poetry in a Glass

With every pour, the stories swell,
Each drop a giggle, a tale to tell.
The glass reflects a riotous cheer,
As flavors mingle, the laughter nears.

A splash of daring, a swirl of fun,
While grapes invite the evening sun.
With little sips, the joy ignites,
In mouthfuls of whimsy, pure delights.

The bubbles dance, they jump and play,
Sipping wine, we chase the gray.
With aromatic whispers in the air,
Each round pours forth a jovial flair.

So raise your glass, let worries pass,
In liquid dreams, we'll never pass.
With every clink, our laughter flows,
In joyful ripples, the spirit grows.

Beneath the Harvest Skies

Beneath the harvest skies, they say,
The grapes hold secrets in a playful way.
They wiggle and giggle as they grow,
Dreaming of a dance before the show.

A squirrel with style, a raccoon in tune,
Join the grape party beneath the moon.
With hats made of leaves, they surely wear,
A harvest ball, oh, the sweet debonair!

The farmers laugh, quite in disbelief,
As their grapes tease them with every leaf.
They plot and scheme, oh what a fuss,
To please the bunches, they're in a rush!

At dusk, they prance on teetering vine,
Each one boasting, "I taste just fine!"
In barrels they dream, as night takes flight,
Vowing to age, but staying up all night!

Spirits of the Soil

In the soil where secrets hide,
The spirits dance, oh, what a ride!
With worms as trumpets, and roots for feet,
They gather 'round for a funky beat.

They chant of harvest, with a wink and a nudge,
A plot thickens, they won't budge!
The critters sway and share their lore,
Of grapes so juicy, they beg for more.

"Mud masks for all!" a grape did shout,
"Let's celebrate—get the barrel out!"
With laughter echoing through each row,
Sprits of the soil put on quite a show.

As dawn breaks softly, the giggles tease,
The grapevine whispers in the morning breeze.
Though serious connoisseurs might not agree,
The soil's spirits dance wildly, just to be free!

A Palette of Pinot

With a palette of Pinot in playful bloom,
Each grape a color—a jolly costume.
They roll and tumble, a vibrant spree,
Painting barrels with zest and glee.

A chubby little grape slipped on a rind,
"Watch me!" he squealed, his friends lined behind.
They took a leap, a fruity parade,
In a splash of juice, their laughter cascades.

"Let's blend the reds with a splash of green,
A fruity fusion like none you've seen!"
They each tried a swirl, a daring sip,
"More bubbles, please!" they cried with a flip.

As corks popped off, they cheered the cheer,
"Mistakes bring joy; let's all raise a sphere!"
In the glassy laughter, they twinkled bright,
A barrel of fun under soft twilight.

Nectar's Refrain

In the vines where nectar flows like dreams,
Grapes hum a tune with silly themes.
They swing like swallows on a sunny spree,
Whispering secrets in glee-filled decree.

"Let's brew some mischief, a playful clink!"
As bees gather 'round, they wink and wink.
With honey on lips, they break into song,
Where laughter blooms, you can't go wrong.

"Come swirl about, let's tease the air,
With bumps and wobbles, we'll toss our care."
The harvest hummed a merry refrain,
As grapes rolled dice in a jubilant chain.

When twilight dropped its velvet cloak,
They toasted themselves, the grapes, they spoke:
"Here's to the laughter, and a barrel or two,
In nectar's sweet bid, let the mirth ensue!"

Threads of the Vintage

In fields where the grapes twirl and spin,
The farmers dance while the crows dive in.
They drink from the barrel, they spill on the floor,
Claiming the sun is a friend and a bore.

With hats full of grapes and shoes stained with red,
They laugh at the way the old barrels spread.
A piece of the harvest they claim as their prize,
While the birds scold them with judgmental cries.

Autumn brings laughter, a crisp in the air,
With jokes about vines that are starting to care.
The squirrels hold council on how to invade,
Each nibble of fruit is a plan they have made.

Bottles uncorked like a dragon's breath,
Spitting out bubbles while dancing with death.
The corks fly high like confetti in glee,
Who knew grape juice could tickle so free?

With every sip comes a giggle, a cheer,
As the winemaker tells tales too wild for the ear.
So raise your glass high, let your spirits take flight,
In the world of the foolish, all's perfectly right.

Essence of the Autumn Sky

Beneath the vast hues of orange and gold,
The grapes do a tango, if truth be told.
With the sun on their backs, they're a little bit tipsy,
Declaring themselves the most fruity and frisky.

The wind whispers secrets and ruffles the leaves,
While the vines conspire with mischievous thieves.
They giggle and wiggle in shadows so sly,
As neighbors complain to the clouds up high.

Every harvest moon brings a festival loud,
Where the grapes leap around, feeling oh-so-proud.
Their sense of adventure is humble yet grand,
With juice on their cheeks and crush on demand.

With laughter ripe like the fruit they produce,
They toast to the season in loud, joyous use.
"Here's to the clouds that rain without care,
And hope for more sunshine, if they want to share!"

Embracing the fog that frolics and flirts,
The grapes shake their stems in beautiful skirts.
A quirky parade in the chill of the night,
Where autumn's bright glow keeps the laughter in sight.

Voids and Vines

In the land of the twists and the daring green climbs,
The grapevines gossip in their own little rhymes.
With roots that are ticklish and leaves that conspire,
They dream of the sun and a life that's much higher.

The soil is a party, a rave with no end,
Where worms are the dancers, and bugs are the friends.
They swirl in a frenzy, they laugh 'til they cry,
As the old oak tree rolls its wizened old eye.

"To ferment or not?" asked the grape with a grin,
"Let's jest with the barrels, let the fun begin!"
While corks fly and pop like the jokes from above,
The bottles all giggle, a true labor of love.

The harvest is booming, the barrels are packed,
While slip-ups and mishaps leave laughter intact.
In this rowdy circus where silly thrives best,
Even the winemaker forgets all the stress.

So gather your friends and let spirits run free,
Raise a glass to the voids, to the vines and the glee.
In the chaos of joy, let's share in the cheer,
For life's just a blend of good wine and good beer.

Perfumed Paths

With hints of aromas that weave through the air,
The grapes play hide-and-seek without a care.
As blossoms embrace with scents oh-so-fine,
They giggle and roll down the soft-sloped incline.

The sun throws a party, the clouds dance too,
With laughter erupting like morning dew.
As shadows bounce happily across the old grass,
The fruit conspire boldly: "Just let the day pass!"

Among tangled trellises, joy finds its way,
The bees join the dancing, and sweet songs they play.
With hiccups and hiccups, the grapes plot and scheme,
Their essence igniting this sweet little dream.

So grab your old bottle, uncork all that cheer,
Join the revelry, for the harvest is near.
Together we laugh, let our spirits uplift,
In the dance of the vines, happiness is gift.

With jests and with japes, the days slip away,
As summer bids farewell at the end of the day.
The sweetness of life flows in every fine drop,
In this world of absurdity, let the laughter not stop.

The Symphony of Seasons

The grapes in winter, dressed in snow,
They ponder life, what do they know?
When summer comes, they sizzle and pop,
In sunny attire, they dance on top.

The fall brings laughter, leaves of gold,
Grapes cracking jokes, never too old.
They toast to the frost, with a giggle and squeeze,
While squirrels steal snacks, with deft little knees.

As springtime unfolds, the blossoms appear,
Grapes gossip softly, while sipping their beer.
Each season a note in this quirky refrain,
They revel and frolic, no hint of disdain.

Together they play in this rowdy delight,
With laughter and chatter from morning to night.
The chorus of colors, a comical scene,
The grapes on their journey, living the dream!

Embrace of the Elms

Under the elms, they swing and sway,
Grapes gossip freely, keeping boredom at bay.
They plan a trip, to the sunlit shores,
Where juice-filled laughter is all that pours.

One grape says, "Hey! Let's play hide and seek!"
Another replies, "Or dance like a freak!"
They stumble and roll, all in good fun,
Chasing each other, till the day is done.

With roots intertwining, they form a big hug,
Whispering secrets, snug as a bug.
They dream of adventures, of plans oh so grand,
While sipping on sunshine, hand in hand.

The elms nod in rhythm, a green leafy cheer,
For grapes and their antics that bring so much cheer.
Under the sun, in the warm, cozy light,
The elms join the party, oh what a sight!

Sunkissed Dreams

On a bright day, grapes melt in the sun,
Whispering dreams, can we have some fun?
They dream of being all fruity and fine,
While sneaking a sip of that sugary wine.

One plump grape laughed, "Look at me glow!"
While another replied, "Just don't let it show!"
They twirled and they swayed, in a fruit parade,
With visions so silly, they just can't fade.

As the sun sets low, they gather in packs,
Time for tall tales, with no holding back.
With stories of pluck, and sweet summer treats,
They giggle and chuckle at their tasty feats.

From whimsy to wonder, each grape is a star,
During this sunset parade, oh so bizarre!
With dreams on the vine, and laughter in seams,
Their spirits fly high, all sunkissed in beams!

Portrait of a Winemaker

A winemaker strolls with a curious grin,
Sampling the grapes, where the fun begins.
With each little sip, a new tale to weave,
Inked in the laughter, on nights that deceived.

Deadlines approach, and the grapes start to squish,
He dances with barrels, making a wish.
In the midst of the crush, they laugh and they spill,
His dream is a blend of chaos and thrill.

With corkscrew winks and bottle cap games,
He juggles the vintages, calling their names.
Each barrel a canvas, each bottle a tune,
A symphony crafted beneath the bright moon.

He swirls and he sniffs, with a grin on his face,
Each drop tells a story, with unique grace.
So raise up a glass to this whimsical man,
Who's captured the nectar with a cheeky plan!

www.ingramcontent.com/pod-product-compliance
Lightning Source LLC
Chambersburg PA
CBHW051635160426
43209CB00004B/651